**Incendium
Amoris**
Steve Ely

STACK
BOOKS

Smokestack Books
1 Lake Terrace, Grewelthorpe, Ripon HG4 3BU
e-mail: info@smokestack-books.co.uk
www.smokestack-books.co.uk

ISBN 978-0-9955635-5-1

Smokestack Books is
represented by Inpress Ltd

Super aspidem & basiliscum ambulabis : & conculcabis leonum & draconem. ¶On *the* snake and *the* basilisk*e thou* sall ga : and *thou* sall defoul *the* lyon and *the* dragon. ¶ *The* snake werpis, and *the* tade nuryssis *the* eg. and *thar*of is broght forth *the* basilysk*e. that* is kald kygn*e* of serpents. for a white spot is in his heuyd *that* makis hi*m* to seme as he had a dyademe on. his stynkand smell slas serpents. his ande foghyls *that* fleghis abouen hi*m*. his syght all lifand thynge. bot *that the* wesill ou*er*cu*m*ys hi*m* and slas hi*m*. *the* snake is ill eggynge *that* hurtis men pri*u*ely ar *th*ai wit, and w*ith* delyte and assentyng*e* till syn bri*n*gis forth the basilysk. *that* is, grete synne in dede, *that with the* sight slays all *the* v*er*tus of *the* saule : w*ith* stynkand smell of ill ensau*m*pill slas me*n that* cumes nere : and w*ith* ill ande. *that* is, w*ith* venymous worde slas *the* herers : bot *the* vesyll. *that* is, *the* rightwisman. *that* gas *thar*on gastly, and slas it. and swa he defouls vndir*e* his fete of goed will. *the* lyou*n. that* is, all cruelte till his neghbur*e*. and *the* dragou*n, that* is, gilry. and pri*u*e malice, *that* blou*n*diss w*ith the* heuyd &smytes w*ith the* tayle.

Richard Rolle, *Commentary on the Psalter, Psalm XC: 13*

Contents

Officium

Old Street

Midnight dog fox marking blood; Pound's phantom
hellhounds, the occult consultancy
of Leo Africanus. Flashback, subliminal vision:
Catweazle in cuccula, somehow it's me;
ash wand, lantern, psalter and snares.
Timeslip gleaners on Love Balk stubbles;
did I see them or dream them? The witch
at Bilham Row; definitely dream. The hermit's cell
in Hampole Wood; windflower, pilewort,
curve of the exposed stromatolite reef.
Science. Owlet in bluebells, endymion non-scripta.
Asiotic night screams horned like Cernunnos –
we like that kind of noise.

Catweazle

Catweazle in cuccula, dynamiting windfarms
and chopping barbed wire. Joey Bach and Malc Spencer,
slipping lurchers and love-notes to keepers.
Malc's sister's a medium; Dad's looking down,
with the dogs – and dog-fox, Leo Africanus.
Cross on Lound Lane – *Patris, Filii, et Spiritus Sancti.*
Catweazle in cuccula, gay Richard dour
in sister's kirtle. The holly bower
in Fishponds Wood, KY and Paco Rabanne.
Sister at Hampole, cottaged in rape
of the Priory. Cunt books in hedgerows.
Richard and Margret, couchant in bushes –
asiotic night screams horned like Cernunnos.

Jerusalem

Pathfinder – Doncaster, Dearne. Old Street
in Elmet, from Strafford to Tanshelf via Beacon.
And did those feet? Agricola, Hengist,
the ceorl in charge of the king's gerfalcon.
Muck between the toes, Holy Communion.
Cross on Lound Lane at the fork to Rat Hall,
forward to Hampole and Watlynge Street.
Stump-scratting in bluebells with metal detectors,
endymion non-scripta. Rusted shire-shoe,
crown of the witch-pricking king. Skrying in wheel ruts
and livers of badgers. Deerhounds hammering
lazerlit pastures. Yommer with spade
and crowbar. Brock-rotted stromatolite reef.

Bloen

Badger Balk, the tinkers' exiled grazeway.
A.K.A. Lenny. Broad Balk, the cart-road
to Red House. Love Balk from Redroof
to Rat Hall and Pigburn. Bread Walls
Broadrick, Bluegate Flatt; Catweazle in cuccula,
somehow it's me, a peach-cheeked mendicant,
stockinged in partridge. Shotgun discharge,
Ghost of a Flea; overalls, labrador,
Baikal over-and-under – *And did those feet?*
Fled to the tumblestone cottage of potions;
dog fox, hellhounds, Leo Africanus.
She lay on me like brock-pelt, greasy as weasel.
Lips found her nipples, familiar.

Ostentatio Vulnerum

Wind farms and hedgeflails. Glyphosate sterilisation.
Land and landscape abandoned to looters,
surrendered like the Church. Lucy and Margot,
nuns of roofless Hampole, look out
on gleaners of Deep Dale stubbles
and finger their rosy beads; boar-tusk,
bear-claw, clavicle of hare. Panicking magpies,
Larsen trapped, tempting down buzzards;
FarmStar, Greensleeves, Good Energy PLC,
ploughing blood and reaping gold.
Catweazle in Realtree cuccula, conjuring Aske,
Yommer and Malc. Joey's single-shot. 410.
God's wounds. Turbine flea'd in rooks.

Sweoster

Obliterate ruin of Hampole Priory:
wagtail farmyard, root barn roofed with rats.
Housewarmed in ashlar salvaged from transepts.
Catweazle pre-cuccula, gulling gormless guests
with ghosts: the boy who fell through the ice
of the carp pond. Christmas Day, black monks
carousing, deaf to the drowner's screams;
'to this day' his wet and weedy footprints
stalk the festive street. The story's fatal flaw:
Luterel's sisters, Margret of Kyrkeby;
the Priory was a *nunnery*. Fake spirits
and plausible dreamers: dog fox, hellhounds,
Leo Africanus. Cromwell, Ghost of a Flea.

Pastoral

By his cell, used condom and rotovated earth;
elbow-dents, arse-rut, discarded tampon,
a drained half-bottle of rum. Horned
like Cernunnos, Richard is naked,
pissing up a tree. His psalter is warm
and awry – *every beast of this forest is mine.*
Margret rolls like a dog in soapy bracken,
renewing her virginity. Oak crowns swelling
and rifting. Jays screeching overhead.
Smirking swineherd whistling through, broad front
of pigs at pannage. Dick pats her dry
with her untressed hair and orders her habit.
Her gret papys yet tremble and lift to his touch.

Hampull Wood

Greenfly clotting the spider's web, crusting
like mould. Silk strands stretching and sagging
out of shape, snapping under load. She strings
her cables, patient as the cross. Stags rutting
under plantains, cloister of scuttering blackclocks.
Dragons hunt the ride as though trained along wires,
bolts of flaming sapphire. Thrush swells like a dumpling;
the flecks on her breast are hearts and tears.
Woodcock in shadow and woodcock in sun
are almost different birds, probing the churnings
of shovel-snecked boars, the heaped fumes of bears.
Night Prayer lit by the eyes of wolves,
their heave of breathing, and smoking breath.

Rapture

A muck-floored shack of plough-turned field-stone,
lit by tallow candles – Richard's scriptorium.
Christ on the cross, the Vulgate of St. Jerome.
Swan wings hanging from roof laths,
piles of creamy parchment. Cut quills and blæc;
soot and honey, heat and sweetness scribing song.
In winter's field is the Fellowship of Angels;
Michael, Gabriel, Thrones and Dominions.
I fall in with the love choir; the roaring of bears,
the bellowing of boars, the howling of wolves.
Rum, ram, raf. This polyphony is me.
Lego Latine, scribo Latine,
in Anglicus cogito. In Englisc ic singe.

To Mega Therion

Nights can be difficult. Snuffling pigs
and racing martens keep me from sleep,
owl-shriek, concupiscent dreams, torrid
and incontinent. I wake to the Beast,
horned like Cernunnos, and flee to the Name of Jesus.
The cockcrowed heaven is dizzy with angels,
venite exultemus domino. Dawn streaking
from the East, and Lucifer rising. Creation
clamours in song. I break bread and give thanks,
for my friend the redbreast, tamed by crumbs to hand.
I shit in the woods, then wash in Margery's pail.
She comes at none, when the forest is quiet.
I sit and sing and write and rove and play.

Banquet of Virgins

What drove me to this solitude?
I dare not confront it. I absent my desert
for women, sometimes food and wine.
These I confess. Words gush like fleet Ea,
yet I have but one thing to say: turn your back
on this world and worship His Name; wash
in His blood and be saved. Seduced, we embrace,
over and over, heat and sweetness, song.
I am your Father and you my monkish girl.
We sit knee-to-knee, handfast in yearning.
You confess you are often tempted,
as am I. Your green eyes glitter like a cat's.
Sometimes your penance is submission.

The harpe, and the voice of a Psalme

Which is better, to preach, or to love?
To dispute and expound, or to feel?
The prideful puff their proofs from pulpits,
rum, ram, raf. This carnal world is their reward;
they descend to the Devil by diploma
and degree. The meek inherit the Kingdom,
though they flee from the malice of ministers
and monks. The fire of love incinerates sin:
in fullness of flame I am blent in bliss
and thus made perfect; and God would have you
perfect too. Feel the warmth of his embrace,
taste the honey of his tongue. *Syngis til the lord
a new sange: for in thee he will make woundirs.*

Pilgrimage of Grace

Officium et miracula. He raised the dead.
What else? Broadcast wolf's teeth,
stony rubble, Deep Dale's turbined field.
They formed as men from Barnsdale's earth
and clots of Becket's blood. And walked.
Cutting cudgels from the coppice,
commandeering horse, they marched on Megiddo,
bannered in Wounds. Dreams sainted
with vision and strange synchronicity.
Catweazle in cuccula, Ghost of a Flea.
Golgonooza of terror and healing – *And did those feet?*
Scrubbers at the lists on horsemeat ponies,
tilting at Zetors, nephilim, windmills.

Miracula

Paterfamilias Rogerus, of Hampole

And he that schal falle on this stoon, schal be
brokun; but on whom it schal falle, it schal
al tobrise hym.
Matheu, XXI: 24

A slab from quarry at Stubbs.
Hauled from tumbril, tackle
snagged, and snapped: it dropped
like a hawk – *sweet Saint Richard!*

And rose like a lark, setting itself
in place on tomb. Roger dabbed
small blood and crossed himself –
a cartload of lead, a hairstreak's wing.

Flame fraying to mouldwarp
darkness. Beeswax wilting.
Choir glowing like a stove.
Fen-wolf, distant: compline's descant.

Hugo of Fyselake

Therfor thei token Jeremye, and castiden
hym doun in to the lake of Elchie, [...]
wherynne was no watir, but fen; therfor
Jeremye yede doun in to the filthe.
Jeremye, XXXVIII: 6

Followed the football, fell.
Face-down black muck,
sucked black water:
askr, flittermouse, tade.

Hole in Cuthbert's earth,
a small one: Mamma pumping
his chest and shrieking
to Mary, swiping off worms.

The undertaker's rule: two cubits,
a candle for Richard. Lauds,
the light extinguished –
her dead boy quacking like a duck.

Iohanna of Sprotburgh

Lord, saue vs; we perischen.
Matheu, VIII: 25

Drowned thieving from fish-traps.
Gaffed to the bank
by punting bargees –
glass-eyed, gaping.

Swan-complected, scabbed with leeches,
oozing like the fen.
Maids tore weeds
and wailed to Richard.

She hiccoughed a frog;
eels squirming from her petticoats.
In Hampull's chapel,
her guttering candle flared.

Iohannes of Sutton

Effeta, [...] Be thou openyd.
And anoon hise eris weren
openyd.
Mark, VII: 34-35

Sunday disco, Hacienda:
mirrorball, Hazell Dean,
drink-drive XR3 –
searchin, lookin for love.

Gary Davies back-perm DJ –
oooh. Mandy does/Mandy doesn't;
back-room snooker, potting
the brown and the pink.

What? Puking by the bins.
She sucked her finger
and poked it in my ear –
better move on down the line.

Isabella of Auston

Nether this man synnede, nether
hise eldris; but that the werkis
of God be schewid in hym.
Joon, IX: 3

Wall-eyed Belle, mad
as a sheepdog. The good one,
wholemeal partridge;
the oddball, starling-blue.

Widowed and witchy, drawing
looks and slander, walking
into doors. She needed a man,
and threw herself on Richard:

who understood her agony,
prostrated on his tomb;
her joy as moon-pie split
to vision, glossy as a conker.

The Paralytic of Wrangbroke

Ryse vp, take thi bed, and go in
to thin hous.
Mark, II: 11

Dirt-track junction, snarling
quadbikes. Cigs, Lambrini,
TLC – Cake Boss,
Bride Wars, Tit-job Dreams.

Richard in hermit's habit,
advert usurping – *seemples!*
Up she stood, put her foot
through the flatscreen.

A miracle! Tell the neighbours,
he said. She entered the Brookside
fun run. That was a laugh.
Even the winners were cripples.

Thomas of Morehows

For thou, Lord, liytnest my lanterne;
my God, liytne thou my derknessis.
Psalms, XVIII: 29

Ague from stank, or Satan:
in truth, we are infants,
knowing nothing. But writhe
did my legs like serpents.

And vomited. Flesh sweating
like cheese. Three days,
three nights – *alma redemptoris*
mater – save me.

So little the Saint needs:
two pounds of wax
from Hampole's hives – the kiss
of his fingers, warm as comb-honey.

Willelmus filius Radulphi

Thei schulen do awei serpentis;
and if thei drynke ony venym,
it schal not noye he.
Mark, XVI: 18

He drove the cattle from the corn
and roared onto the common.
Lad blue among anthills,
quivering like a windflower.

Three days he sweated on his pallet,
eyes rolling like cauldron dumplings;
until they swore by the Virgin
to give thanks at Richard's tomb.

Whereupon he sat up. And the wesil
slew the adder in the shelduck's cave,
sucking his goldpots – smashed
alabaster, whorled in groping muck.

Bodleian
MS Rawlinson
D. 913

I syng of a lad

I syng of a lad
the joy of Middle-earth
leaven of Our Lady's wombe
a lad of wit and worth.

His houngrie moueth did suck
the tight bud of her breste
there in the cowshed's muck
beneath the swallow's nest.

His hammered thumb did drip
upon his fader's bench
his moder sucked the rip
the squirting blud to quench.

His vivid breth did quicken
partridges of clay
freed from erthe's cold prision
by grace of God's Lady.

His word did conjure wiyn
from wells of Galilee
first-fruits of the vyne
grafted from Marie.

His forehead scored to bone
by gouging Coroun of Thornes
she pled at Pilat's throne
and wepte for her new-borun.

His sunburnt skin did tear
at every flagrant lash
screaming drowned her preyeres
blud sprayed like nettle rash.

His carcase hooked like meat
dripping from the tree
thanksgiving at his feet
his modir Our Lady.

His fell flesh conquered dethe
five wounds healed to holes
from tomb her baby's brethe
swete wind for bitter souls.

I syng of a lad
Lord of Heuene and Earth
bairn and God and manne all three,
Marie's Virgyn birth.

Wulf in weald

Foxis han dennes, and briddis
of heuene han nestis, but mannus
sone hath not where he schal
reste his heede.
Matheu, VIII: 20

Wulf in weald
whelps new-born
blind and ceald
beast of blood and bone.

Bear on haeth
old and alone
winter's wrath
beast of blood and bone.

Eofor in holt
snorting loam
droppèd by bolt
beast of blood and bone.

Hart in hyrst
from houndis flown
haggard and hurt
beast of blood and bone.

Heland in heuene
corsand under stone
man born of woman
beste of blood and bone.

I have a yong whippet

I have a yong whippet
off Baz from Brierley
much is the mete
she has brought to me.

She broghte me the henn
from the five-bar gate
and so she ded the catte
from the Barratt Estate.

She brought me the pheasant
from Little John's Well
and so she did the ræt
from the sewerage by the Skell.

She broghte me the rabbit
from Shotgun Johnson's croft
and so she did the squirrel
from the rafters of the loft.

She broghte me the hare
from Hollins on the chalk
and so she did the roo
from the rape by Badger Balk.

She plucked the fluting blackbird
from the privet in the park
and tore the bleating pigeon
from its grip on the bark.

She bit out Charlie's snowy throat
pulled owls from dry stone walls
did for weasel, foulmart, stoat
chopped mouldwarp, shrew and vole.

She needs no permission
I've practised our story
my lytle bitch
takes all legal quarry.

I have a yong whippet
off Baz from Brierley
moch is the meat
she has broghte to me.

Were in weald lay

Were in weald lay
in weald lay
fortyniht, full fortyniht
were in weald lay.
In weald lay
Fortynighte and a day.

Wanton was his went
honeysuckle's scent
pocket poke and creeper's cleft
wanton was his went.

Wounding was his woe
natterjack and crow
stinkhorn and sphincter
wounding was his woe.

Weapons were his work
dagger of the Turk
adder's tongue and Baldr's bane
weapons were his work.

Wisdom was his worth
dog-fox run to earth
roebuck in the applegarth
wisdom was his worth.

Wonders were his wone
wolf-lord on his throne
bear upon the fallow bitch
wonders were his wone.

Were in weald lay
in weald lay
fortyniht, full fortyniht
were in weald lay.
In weald lay
Fortynighte and a day.

Richard lay a-weeping

Richard lay a-weeping
weeping in his cell
parish priest and prioress
had him condemned to hell
and all was for a cherry
a cherry that he took
of Margaret of Kyrkeby
down by Ea brook.

Had not that cherry take ben
her cherry taken ben
ne had busty Margaret
sung forth like the wren.
Blessed be my lusty Dick
thus says his ancrene whore
the sweetness of the song we sang
his best miracula.

Flame

A Surfeit of Jelly Beans

Trophy was the bitter, the big-headed pint
that thinks it's a quart. I was full of it,
bleached hair, painted leather, the ruffs and frills
of a Restoration dandy. I switched
to the beau monde's cocktail of choice, vodka
and Pernod, topped-off with sugary black.
By Auld Lang Syne I was lurching puff-cheeked
for the exit, wrestling revellers aside.
I didn't make it, puking sweet purple
over her shoulder, before falling through the door
to chuck-up my guts on the salt of the frozen car park.
She staggered me home over ice-rut pavements,
over and over repeating her number,
which my wasted heart remembered, and now I forget.

The Jacket

We read our banns to strangers, in grip
of gormless love. Our idiot rapture
seduced the streets to smiles: we showered
in confetti of bemused congratulation.

Sipping childish cider in shit-hole pubs,
barmaids called us love's young dream
and told us get a room. But heaven and earth
could not contain the fervour of our passion.

Gallant I gave her my envied jacket,
a red leather from X-Clothes in Leeds.
I cloaked it over her flowery shoulders
in a rite of debt and devotion. I would have
given her the world and everything in it –
my love, my honey, my harp. I gave her away.

Shooting Stars down Peggy Lines

His mistress was by no means coy. Not backwards
at coming forwards, by hint or glint
or lingering finger, brush of the back
of the hand. She intended to be taken,
or in lieu of that, to take, but her ingénue
was frozen chaste in pedestalled yearning.
She could not move him from her mouth
even to blouse's button-popped breast.

At midnight on the starry embankment
she took matters in cold, unshrinking hand,
preamble to slime of hot frost on bare buttocks,
fury of flesh, arching back and splayed knees:
not this cross-legged consolation of weeping
centaurids, the first snowdrops of the year.

The Meadow

Imagining her the bride of my heart,
I shared my secret places. Spring Wood
by the antique pack-road, holy well, holly bower,
tumbled-stone bridge; where I buried the baited badger,
cut the rope from the hanged man's tree.
The nests I'd found: little owl, magpie,
bullfinch and turtle. April boasting
narcissi and blackcap's fake philomel.

She knew the wood already, and the 'meadow'
beyond its dry-stone border, having eloped there
one midnight with some cocksure casanova,
easy in his skin, to get fucked among peebeds
and mouldy cowpats, a flushed puit mewing
and dragging her wing, pretending that she's hurt.

Anfortas

Fishing with a limp rod, feeling eels
and lukewarm lampreys. The wound in my thigh
slime of tenches could not heal.
On my suppurating pallet, a waste
of consolation; Juju, von Eschenbach,
The Confessions of Aleister Crowley.
Conduit d'amour, the grail had run dry.
Surgeons, psychiatrists and bags were consulted,
second and smirking third-hand opinions.
The panel reported it all in the mind –
prescribed schoolgirl sluts and kype-lipped salmon.
Pretty perch, bullhead-bumped and tiddler-tickled,
gone fishing with a carbon-fibre Abu Garcia,
foul-hooking ferox and barging barbel.

Japan

Somehow it was my fault – a dole-dossing
androgyne furtive with scandal, stealing
about their midnight landings. *Adolescent sex,*
with juvenile intentions. Her parents believed it:
she and I could only dream. I was forbidden.
She exiled herself to bedsit-land that I might
come around. Did she really? She was running
to her future, risking herself for world.

Loneliness, poverty, resentment and routine;
somehow it was my fault. Deflowered to exultant,
basking relief, I'd drag her from ironing
to the missionary mattress, then leave
for the last bus home. Love became a chore.
The ghosts of my life blow wilder than before.

Down by the river with Clara and Paul

Dripping June. Under Clara's umbrella,
lit by sou'wester and bright yellow raincoat,
unbuttoned in boudoir of wilting bluebells
and engorged rhododendrons.

Milky puffballs in the leaf litter, the blonde
and bleating unhutched weasel. Quivering
pheasants pressed to earth. Cock's head
rising bloody from brambles, battering aloft.

Clara is not satisfied: she is Miriam,
she is Marilyn, sometimes Mary Millington.
To Paul, who is not Paul, but sometimes
would be Baxter, she is Helen – unattainable,
yet nevertheless, attained–and he her fumbling
eunuch Paris. The flowers are smashed.

Eofor

Red bracken and leaf litter
white thighs splay
beneath boarish buttocks
wrist-throats pinned
glimpsed snatch of fox-fur   vixen
squealing pigeons skyward

comes roaring from the brake
the hook-toothed god
of the bristling pizzle
rearing erect and spurting anemones
goring the gaffer
and lording   his lady
humped quivering in the loam.

Paul and Laura Mandragora

Ryse we eerli to the vyner; se we, if the vyner
hath flourid, if the flouris bryngen forth fruytis,
if pumgranatis han flourid; there I schal Yyue
to thee my tetis. Mandrogoris han youe her
odour in oure yatis; my derlying, Y haue kept
to thee alle applis, new and elde.
Cant., VII:12-13

Paul's dick smelled of apples. Laura's apples
smelled of dick. He licked the crinkled berries.
She bit the rooty wick.

Endorphin-doped, Paul sank to sleep, unstrung
Laura dozed, mandrakes tangled in the sheets,
cuffed in pantyhose.

Paul was dazed on methadone, Laura hazed
on smack. The kids were on the internet,
watching Mexican dirt-track.

He dug her mucky garden, she loved
his shovelled earth, drilled with meaty tubers
of man-size length and girth.

Paul forked naked in the loam, Laura hoed
like Eve, rooted in the world's ordure
to which fallen flesh will cleave.

Puppette dragged-up by the hair, Mammette
torn from dreaming, death's bloody aphrodisiac,
nine billion mandrakes screaming.

The Banishing Ritual of the Pentagram

I

Muck-made
in God's image
lit with breath of His name
the law of destruction
reverses creation's rule.
Take His Name from the mouth
truth becomes death
and man blood.

Horsed in flesh
of grinning golem   Adam
weaponed for the quest
burying   drowning
burning   blasting
weaponed for the quest
name or spirit
ἱερόν, a divine thing.

Red gold on crimson gules
Solomon's Seal
perfection in pentads
fingers   senses   joys   and wounds
fraunchyse   fela3schyp
clannes   cortaysye and pité
four limbs of body   the Crown
weaponed for the quest.

Meat artfully knotted
to pentangled bone
Kadmon's golden gematria
cosmografia del minor mondo.
If lies are all we have
make it a good one   meaning
dignity   place   and purpose
spark flaming to pleroma.

II

When God's five-pointed stars plunge-dived from Heaven
they stuck shoulder deep, heads speared in Earth's shit.
Devolution to dirt, legs twitching like leaves
of cabbagy mandrake. Mouse and mouldwarp,
gnawing at the skull-root. Suck of rotting earth.
Suffocate head-spark cooling to crimson and gray.

The daughters of men were fair; they plucked them
kicking and screaming. They scrubbed up well,
as God's sons might; wings like eagles, eyes like flame,
hair like a flock of goats. They built towers
and fed demons in rites of drugged buggery.

God wasn't keen, but reserved His judgement:
let's see where this ends up. Eve split the apple
and Satan her arsecheeks with spunk of the gibbet.
Little Boy, homunculus: golem, destroyer of world.

Fiery and prideful explicatory theorems
pretext for hashish and vas nefandum.
Two fingers to heaven, a goat butting-up.

Every man and woman is a star: Samael,
Lilith, contracted to Cowell via Crowley.

Do what thou wilt be the whole of the law.

III

Ιδέα: candle-head pumpkin-lantern.

Lit rictus, saw-mouthed grin of Devourer:
light extinguished – cold dead flesh-head.

Whose hand lifts lid with flaming Lucifer?
Whose cool breath damps the heat and light?
Something in shadow, seeking not to exist.

Deus absconditus, empyrean skulking.
Serpent in the pit, loosed a little
for Hollywood paedos. Prometheus unzipped
by vultures. Adam Weishaupt? Doctor Yakub?

Bending to lap from the dew pond,
the Monster knew himself,
summoned tailor and barber, a cup
from which to quench his thirst. And threw down
his Master, screaming, *I am no beast.*

They took him apart like a lab-chimp,
screwdrivers, scalpels and binary code.
Fire doused, air burned off and ἱερόνexcised.
Fleshbag-ganglia, herded in appetite,
doped on devouring. Cheetah rattles his cage,
prays for the slaughterer's stun gun.

IV

Rehabilitate pentagram
as Kung fu fighting star,
silver bullet
for Babylon's golem.
hi-YA – for spirit   *hi-YA* – for fire
hi-YA – for air   *hi-YA* – that's water
hi-YA – eat dirt   dirt thou art
to dirt thou shalt return.

The mud-men grow
and destroy creation.
What is their Master?
Something in shadow
seeking not to exist,
seven heads and ten horns
whispering blasphemy
violence against the spirit.

Which cannot name a bird
or tree   delight
in sweet vernal
the quim-stink of fitch
pimps children
to wolfish member.
Rape is the tender
of ambition's high office.

מָה-אֱנוֹשׁ
lower than angels   higher than cattle
chippy knotted on the cross
as Vitruvian Man,
the Spartacists' Golden Ratio.
Crass earth's canon of proportion:
six thousand servile   (Luxemburg, Liebknecht)
broken on stakes   from Berlin to Capua.

Reintroduction of the English Wolf

Six-year-old hipsters in mop cuts and
little-ten Chucks, smack-chic pretty
in dead Kurt's unplugged cardy. Fan-
blather boo-hoo grieving snuffed
celebs on Facebook; flowers at the
foot of the virtual lamp-post, votive
tea lights, libations of Carling and
WKD. Opinions ex nihilo: NHS,
HS2, LGBT; favourite/like/unfriend.
Something for nothing: it's a free
country. *Why* [Brian Cox] *fucking
loves Science* – ME-ME-ME-ME
meme; peer-reviewed selfies and
agitprop preening. Hindmost Acad-
emy, (in)human resource of GB PLC,
fattening youth on fear and ambition,
hysteric for pleasure, advantage.
Airport in the Fen, forest of droning
turbines: ten thousand unit intensive
computerised mechanised dairy-
farm; wrecked tents of Holsteins
sucked dry under UV striplights.
Harrods and Aldi dealing tiger-skin
Ugg boots, Adidas Nitrocharge
crafted from feathers of Slender-
billed curlew: to die for. RSPB
pond-dippers, secure in hard hats and
lifejacket armour, goody-bagged
pizza and Diggerland party: the kids,
for the kids –

HOOOOOOOOOOOOOOOOOOOOOOOOOOOOOOOOOOOWL

Scandalum Cruces

Our age knows [...] what was formerly merely morbid
has today become indecent.
Friedrich Nietszche

I

Sins crying to heaven for vengeance: wilful
murder, the sin of Sodom, oppression of the
poor; defrauding labourers of their wages–
Bangladesh, Barnsley. Clean conscience, fat
wallet, vacs to Dubai, the rings of Saturn and
Bangkok ladyboys. Insurgents licked by
twin-tongued pacifists, ease via aid, armed
intervention. Know them and yourself, and
lie with me.

II

Horses both hobby and high: the Real
Presence of William Warham, Cantuar
sanctuar. Doubleday's muck via Morris and
Kropotkin, ten acres and a cow. Earth dog,
running dog, John Ball's shotgun lectern.
Ocean swollen with sturgeon and cod,
garefowl breaching off Farne. Wapentake
wolfsheads belching in the chamber; roaring
piss-trough, churls passing motions. And
the other place; notarised rights for
screaming mandrakes, United Federation of
Planets.

III

At Cuthbert's shrine I prayed for hair, that
urchins might not mock my pate, that Maria
would drop her drawers.   Perfect God,
nailed to tree imperfect, thus curing man of
sin: mad magic, as opposed to mere magic;
lateral thinking from the mushroomed
yeshiva, perjured to Elohim, the plural
singularity. Elisha commanding she-bears.
Mary, Queen of Heaven. Allegory, analogy;
I'm not sorry for my apology. Nor am I
better than my Fathers. Indulge me, Papa.

IV

I know. That I don't know, or don't know
enough.   Or too much. Reflex sceptic,
reasonable, experienced: calibrate feeling
and bullshit detector; the wild card is
dreaming. The teaching of Phil Smith:
everything is bollocks. The teaching of
Richard Dawkins: *religion is bollocks.*
(Dawkins: subset   of   Smith?)   Smith
insincere: loves his grand-kids and The
Incredible String Band. Insincere, Dawkins?
Loves himself, Christ to Darwin's Baptist.
He coming after me, is preferred before me,
the latchet of whose shoe I am not worthy to
unloose. He's here to end it.

V

Objection one: it's made up. Objection two: it's made up, complicit in murder, etc. Objection three: it's made up, complicit in murder and a hindrance to progress, (etc). Objection four: the priests are nonces. Objective five ... concede, it's likely to be true. Quid est Veritas? Pilate, seeker and sceptic. Scientist? Luther, the worm in Eden's apple. Sola scriptura, discernment flamed by Spirit. Nine billion screaming mandrakes, popes of their piss-poor, privatised pulpits.

VI

What is the Truth? Fire from heaven, stormed Bastilles. Scorched earth and bull-whips. A flag of convenience. That which power permits. Who benefits? Quaere Verum.

VII

Quid est Bonum? Leisure, pleasure, creat-
ivity, control ... four-fold root, insufficient
reason. The rising of the sun and the
running of the deer. Churches built from
England's stone. The dead interred in
England's earth. Cow parsley, foaming
between the graves. Krakers in the barley-
mow, curlews in the corn. News from
Nowhere, the Dream of Gerontius. Christ
on the cross, for me, for you, for Tallis and
Southwell, Langland and Chaucer. *To thee
my God, I will give praise on the harp.* Two
thousand eight hundred and sixty five
frankly impossible things, up-quark, down-
quark, transubstantial gauge boson. *Why
art thou sad, O my soul, and why dost thou
disquiet me?* St. John's on Micklegate, 'The
Parish' – Aftershock, hen-dos, Somebody
Else's Guy. Pete Bucknall supping Smiths:
it's wrong this. Nine billion screaming
mandrakes sticking dildos up their arses.
Quaeret bonum. I know. It ends in failure.

Wealhhnutu

I went downe to the garden of nuttes
To ſe the frutes of the valley, to ſe if the
vine budded , and if the pomegranates
flouriſhed.
Cant.VI:10

I

In the world we won
were foreigners,
the ones who reigned before.
Wealas in the Englisc tunge.
We served them with sword
and serfdom.
Their tafod fled west,
their legacy preserved
in the DNA of concubines,
the shame of their name.

In the world we lost,
the Englisc are the Wealas
of their amnesia and abdication,
the Frankensteined Bryttas
monstered to shopping,
HS2, wind-farms.
Hysterica passio,
magni nominis umbra:
Engle and Seaxe, Wealas ofercoman,
eorlas arhwate, eard begeatan.

Remembrance is resistance
and fancy insurgent.

II

I wept in the valley,
remembering Sion.
The stræt roared with HGVs.
Gulls gloating
out of broken earth,
the plague-pit opened.
Frog in the dry well's throat.
By the tented river,
a withering gibbet of harps.
How shall we sing?

Daughter of Babylon,
happy shall he be
who takes up your little ones
and swings them against the wall,
smashing their skulls like walnuts.
Let the wall's percussion
and damsels' screams
be a song to the Lord
in our estranged land.
If I forget thee, O Jerusalem…

… my voice
has not lost its cunning.

III

Valley of Ea
at calcareous Hampole,
over the river
and electrified railway
from Our Lady's
annihilate Priory.
In a beastless pasture
of shooting ash keys,
the abandoned, alien tree:
wealhhnutu, juglans regia.

South-facing slope
sunbathed by Auster
and gentle Vaturus,
seeded by Caesar from Gaul:
nux gallica,
the unsurrendered,
white-fleshed sapling
of Mary's cloistered garden.
Cneuen Ffrengig,
King of trees.

Ceorls cruching cobs
of sweet Aquila.

IV

Signature of skull,
shell's cranial bone-plates
and florets of kernel
perfectly figuring brain.
Signature of scrotum,
nuts shrunk tight as the sack
of a Tudor rapist, established
by Starkey and R.J. Unstead:
Welsh nutters anointed
dog's bollocks.

Fieldwork at dawn
in Flecktarn combats,
terriers, bars and spades;
Dave Harcombe,
Gildas and Beda.
City of coneys
in osteoporotic Earth.
Trove of humped spoil;
soiled kirtles and psalters,
beads of Whitby jet:

the tourmaline rose
of Lucy de Luterel.

V

Nun-sown walnut, lily of the vale,
trash of wilderness thorns.
I am come in your garden
my sisters, your spouse,
to sing in the shade of your tree.
Ea strums like a lute
in its weirs and bankments
and the taut rails hum like harps.
Will you gather and listen?
And will your ghosts confess?

Will boughs of the walnut
bear fruit of the rope?
Five-wounded Jesus is dead.
Graves on the green:
Lucy, Margaret, Dick.
We set over us strangers
of Anglecynn chosen,
lucred and presumptious:
blind to the skeining cranes
of the chase, deaf to their trumpets.

Price of a dog, a whore's hire.
There will be an accounting.

Wesyll

Stick your fucking wedding ring up your arse.
Sucked a cat's brain through its orbital socket.
Splunk pikejaws of viper, squirmed millipede
ribcage; et out via vulva, the unhinged head.

Shit in the hole. See them fall: Chaz, Lou,
Nick; Reza Pahlavi. They never sin
no one like me; stynkand, shrieking: curling
to sleep between hot breasts cold by morning.

Little Saint Hugh

Lincoln, Friday, 30th July, 1255. The wedding feast of Belaset, Berechiah's daughter. Princes of the Jews from London, Aachen, Strasburg, Worms. *Look at them.* Football on Brauncegate, lads braying their ball against the Jew's stone walls – thump, thump, thump. Fishwives smirking and sneering. Damn your wedding, Jews! Cleric and schoolmaster, shaking their heads. Who knows what secrets behind those walls? The treasures, the blasphemies and perversions?   And the ball sailed high and into the courtyard. Not I. I dare not. Nor I. The footballers frittered away. Save one, little Hugh throwing stones at the Jew's high window. With their gold, and jewels and silver plate, would they have a boy's football, a pig-bladder stuffed with rags?   And at length, dark Belaset came to the window.

> 'Throw down my ball, Jew's daughter
> throw down my ball, will ye?
> I am but a poor English child
> but this toy is dear to me.'

> 'English child, I have your ball
> but I will not throw it down
> from this, my bridal chamber
> in this, my bridal gown –

> 'All through my wedding feast
> that football shook our walls,
> and your insults and profanity
> rang within our halls –

> 'Humbling noble Berechiah
> before his haughty kin
> for the great and good of Jewry
> assembled are within –

'English child, I have your ball:
but perhaps to your surprise
I will indeed return your toy:
if you come in, and apologise.'

'Throw down my ball, Jew's daughter,
I dare not come inside
for as you did to Jesu Christ
You'll do to me, false bride.'

The Jewess laughed with blood-red mouth
and teeth like ivory.
'Oh, child I shall not hurt thee;
come inside and see –

'Jewry's sons are gentil
as he born of Marie
and with our Christian neighbours
seek peace and amity –

'Is not Moses our shared father
who wrote 'thou shalt not kill'?
Myself I would condemn to hell,
if child, I did thee ill –

'Fritters, tarts and gingerbread
are left over from my feast;
I'll treat thee child, give back thy ball
and then I'll thee release.'

'Oh pious and kindly Jewess
I have you slandered carelessly.
Your generous faith has won my trust
I will come in to thee –

'And eat perhaps a tart-de-bry
a dish of creme boylede
before departing with my ball;
I give my thanks to thee.'

The courtyard doors swung open
and there in silk and lace
the Jew's dark and comely daughter,
arms opened in embrace.

The courtyard doors swung open
and Little Hugh walked in.
Those dark doors closed behind him:
he was never seen again.

Lincoln, Friday, 27th August, 1255. The well by Copin the Jew's house. Stench, foul water. Men laddering down to investigate – guts from the fleshammels, a dead dog? Thirty foot down, wedged between the walls: a boy's body. Priest, sexton. The boy's screaming mother. Twenty eight days missing. She knew. *She knew.* Grappled into the light, laid out on the cobbles. *God's wounds!* Side-speared, pierced hand and foot; scalped and scourge-slashed, head peppered with stab-holes; nose and lips cut off. The boy's screaming mother, embracing putrefaction. *THE JEWS!* Crowd-surge, tumult. *They knew. THE JEWS!* Peitevin the Rabbi, peering from his window, then rushing to bar the door. *THE JEWS! THE JEWS!* Men down the well, looking for more bodies. *THE JEWS!* Something flew out – a pig's bladder stuffed with rags. *THE JEWS!*

Copin was dragged to gibbet
at horse-tails.

Peitevin fled.

The King intervened.
He clapped the Jews in irons
and sent them to the Tower,
where they were variously:
        executed;
        expropriated;
        ransomed and returned,
to fulfil God's purpose,

(as explained by Austin and expounded by the Friars),
and earn for the King.

And the Lexinton brothers were in there conniving:
Bishop Harry in hock for the Angel Choir
in need of relief and a saintly earner;
Robert lending sub rosa at 4d in the pound;
and John, that man of 'weight and learning',
'brave and accomplished knight'
inciting for family and Henry's exchequer.

> Here's a thing:
> anti-Semitism came from the King.

It is known that [Henry I, reigned 1100-35] issued a charter of protection to the Jews, or at least to certain individuals. The text of this is now lost, but it was so important that [...] it may be regarded as the fundamental charter of liberties of medieval English Jewry. It guaranteed, above all, liberty of movement throughout the country, relief from ordinary tolls, protection from misusage, free recourse to royal justice and responsibility to no other, permission to retain land taken in pledge as security, and special provision to ensure fair trial. It confirmed the community, in short, in a position of privilege as a separate entity – existing for the king's advantage, protected by him in all legitimate transactions and answerable to him alone. This charter was confirmed by succeeding rulers after their accession, though not gratuitously.
Cecil Roth, *A History of the Jews in England*

A girl of St. Martin's parish prays at the Shrine of Little St. Hugh.

Girl: O Little St. Hugh, why is it our bishop
           tolerates Jewry in our midst, for are we not
           taught that they slew Our Lord and rejected
           His faith, killing His children?

St. Hugh: Child, the Lord chose the Jews from the
nations to hear His revelation; and though,
by rejecting His Christ, they are in most
grievous error (for which they will suffer the
torments of Hell), in respect of God's
choosing we suffer them to live among us.
For scripture teaches that ere our Shepherd's
return, Jewry must gather to His fold.
However, inspired by the Spirit, Holy Church
has decreed that the goats of Gehenna must
separate from His sheep, lest the flock be led
astray.

Girl: O Little St. Hugh, is that why the knights of
the Shire show kindness to the Jews, that
they are obedient to the teachings of Holy
Church? For the Jews try them sorely with
their synagogues and flaunting.

St. Hugh: Indeed girl, the knights are obedient. But
their patience comes of necessity. For to
maintain their manors, they need borrow of
Jewry and pay two hundred and eight
pennies per annum in the pound: else the
Jews will seize their posterity.

Girl: O Little St. Hugh, will not the King protect
his knights from Jewry's greed and malice?

St. Hugh: Innocent child, the King must uphold the
teachings of the Lateran Palace. Thus he
may not maim Jewry without cause; and his
knights *are* ambitious. Yet the King uses his
Jews for their lucre, which he will have for
his court, his palaces and wars.

Girl: O Little St. Hugh, will not the King, his
knights and bishops, protect his people
from Jewry, their murders and arrogance?

St. Hugh: When Jewry's coffers are emptied, then
            shall he protect thee.

Girl: Yet the commons want, and are restless.

St. Hugh: They are sinners, burning for feast and riot.
            Their Lords will chastise them, and use as
            they will.

Girl: O Little St. Hugh, let them turn from sin
            and be used well.

Both: Amen.

When the king was [...] resident in the parts beyond the sea, many
people in the county of York took an oath together against the Jews,
being unable to endure their opulence while they themselves were
in want; and, without any scruple of Christian conscientiousness,
thirsted for their perfidious blood, through the desire of plunder.
Those who urged them on [...] were certain persons of higher rank,
who owed large sums to those impious usurers [...] the whole class
of workmen, and all the young men in the city, with a very great
mob of country people, and not a few military men, assisted with
such alacrity, and urged forward the work of blood, as if each one
sought his own private advantage [...] those who had previously
regarded the Jews with hatred, [...] openly and with unbridled
license began to rage against them; and, not being content with
their substance, they gave to [them] the option either of holy
baptism, or of death.
William of Newburgh, *Historia rerum Anglicarum*

> and they sought to stick his head on a pole because
> *everywhere we go* and wheeled out trolley loads of
> flatscreens and lager *people wanna know* and set fire
> to the burger van *who we are* and went at it on the
> beach with mods and rockers *shall we tell em* and
> threw a granny off the pier for a laugh *in-ger-land in-*

ger-land in-ger-land and smashed up the spar and stamped on the manager's head because *we're the yorkshire republican army we're barmy where ever we go we fear no foe* and ten thousand feathercuts chanting *you're gonna get your fucking heads kicked in* butchered frogs in the southwark stews *here-we-go here-we-go here-we-go* five hundred swinging on the fences of the tennis courts at minsthorpe *we're not going back we're not going back* goths *going home in a fucking ambulance* smethhurst and mosley loving their neighbour *you black bastard you black bastard* jamie jones to the lads from the salford academy I'll not keep you long because you'll want to get back for some looting *I found an old stocking and filled it with lead/I hit an old woman right over the head/a copper came up to me and asked me my name/so I scarred him for life with a bicycle chain*   a revel

And the land shall yield her fruit, and ye shal eat your fill, and dwell therein in safetie [...] and if thy brother bee waxen poore, and fallen in decay with thee, then thou shalt relieve him, yea though he be a stranger or a soiourner, that hee may liue with thee.
Leviticus, XXV: 19, 35

Grain swells in fragrant
arable; bulls beefed
on buttercup leys.
Fleece-dropped
Lincolns, sweetening
on saltmarsh.
Double-yoke churn-cream
baked in custards.
Slavering sighthounds,
ear-dragged hares.

Abundance of nature, the whole –

Sport and dancing, beer.

> Abundance of nature, the whole
> folk –

Eden
on George-Hill
laden tables
John Ball and Wat Tyler   Leopold of Siena

> Abundance of nature, the whole
> folk

behind it

Ash-root brock-hole glowing
with gold. Worm brooding
hoard like shelduck – *nachash*

Nithhogg   chiselling
the ashroot
gnawing Rialto's piles – *neschek*

nachash   נָחָשׁ   *serpent*

neschek [sic]   נֶשֶׁךְ   *biter*

underneath the lot

Where rats appear, they bring ruin by destroying mankind's goods and foodstuffs. In this way, they spread disease, plague, leprosy, typhoid fever, cholera, dysentery, and so on. They are cunning, cowardly and cruel and are found mostly in large packs. Among the animals, they represent the rudiment of an insidious, underground destruction.
Der Ewige Jude, Dir. Fritz Hippler

poor yitts pay Stinkschuld's price
　　　a few big jEWS　　real jEW super-neschek
('not narrowly racialist', because that would be a sin
worse than genocide – *bad taste,*
the fine calibrations of Fitzroy eugenics
debased to cosh-carrying cock-er-nee prejdiz),
Sassoon and Shylock, Ikey Solomon,
　　　squeezing shire-blood to matzot
　　　from Agincourt to Austerlitz, Mafeking,
　　　Flanders, Helmand Province –

　　　nESCHEK of Lincoln,
asset-stripped to Westminster's
saccarium Aaronis
for Richard to piss up the walls of Jerusalem
and John to dump in the Wash

lEO of York　　　dAVID of Oxford
('L̷eo & 'D'avid, 2nd. Ed.)
bled white by Henry's tallage
the punctured corpse of Little Saint Hugh
　　　bled white by Henry's tallage.

*As the canon law did not apply to Jews, these were not liable to
the ecclesiastical punishments which were placed upon usurers by
the popes, Alexander III in 1179 having excommunicated all
manifest usurers. Christian rulers gradually saw the advantage of
having a class of men like the Jews who could supply capital for
their use without being liable to excommunication, and the money
trade of western Europe by this means fell into the hands of the
Jews. They were freed from all competition, and could therefore
charge very high interest, and, indeed, were obliged to do so owing
to the insecure tenure of their property. In almost every instance
where large amounts were acquired by Jews through usurious
transactions the property thus acquired fell either during their life
or upon their death into the hands of the king. This happened to
Aaron of Lincoln in England, Ezmel de Ablitas in Navarre, Heliot*

de Vesoul in Provence, Benveniste de Porta in Aragon, etc. It was
for this reason indeed that the kings supported the Jews, and even
objected to their becoming Christians, because in that case they
could not have forced from them money won by usury.
'Usury', Jewish Encyclopedia.com.

Borsch-belt tummler
D.D. Kaminsky
expounding insight
of Hans *Christian* Andersen
mediated through Marx
and Magna Carta:

> *'Look at the King! Look at the King!*
> *Look at the King, the King, the King!'*

Neschek of diadems
and fasces, big-biter
of ballot box – whited
werewolf, savaging his fold.
Nachash, shapeshifter,
shedder of skins:
Edward Jew-hammer,
church-wrecking Henry
and Beliar the inciter,
flat-rock basking
by Caesar's pool,
his legion banking
numbers ex nihil;
tongues flickering
quims of teenage whores.

'Inch worm, inch worm
Measuring the marigolds
Seems to me you'd stop and see
How beautiful they are.'

But two-and-two are sixty-four
Four-and-four, five-hundred-and-eight –
exponential increase
of gold and silver plate.

The rich man in his castle
Jew driven from his gate
exiled to Pale's shtetl
cursed and expropriate.

'That poor little ugly duckling
Went wandering far and near
But at every place they said to his face
Get out, get out of here.'

Hurled from the Rock are our Princes
The learned, the wealthy, the fair:
Stripped of their glorious raiment,
Exposed to the fowl of the air.

Who will bewail them, the perfect,
All crowned with the Crown of the Law,
Reared up on scarlet and purple
To study the book without flaw?

(Rabbi Menahem ben Jacob, of Worms, after the 1190 York pogrom.)

How do you do,
Little Saint Hugh?
How many Jews
were butchered for you?

Kicking your ball
against Wannsee's wall
Nürnberg and Hertha
drawing two-all.

The plaza melee
first one up to three
heralds proclaiming
the Alhambra decree.

Shirts v. skins
next goal wins.
Chişinău clips
Maccabi's wings.

But don't bring complaint
to the infant Saint.
He was but the Gazza
of the streets of St. Mazza.

Found dead in a well.
How? Who can tell?
Probably after his ball –
be-all and end-all.

And on Brauncegate's cobbles,
Ardiles and Hoddle;
Kluivert and Cruijff,
from Amsterdam Oost.

Jumpers for posts
streets packed with ghosts
come to see Rocket Ron
and Avi Cohen.

The jubilee starts
Agoos to Sjaak Swart
into blond Voronin
wide to J.P. Sorin

whipped to back stick
Hugh's bicycle kick
breaking the net:
maybe that clears the debt.

Hugh rips off his shirt
the crowd goes berserk.
Some kid out of Sheol
lobs back the ball,

but it's no Surridge Cobbler
or tuppeny wobbler
but the head of the King –
basilisk, where is thy sting?

Can you hear nachash sing?
  No-o, no-o.
Can you hear nachash sing?
  No-o, no-o.
Can you hear nachash sing?
  I can't hear a fucking thing.
Hsss. Hsss. Hsss.

Je te plumerai

Hreodfenn fallows at Standing Flatt Bridge,
agger of Old Stræt fording the flood.
Ox-teams hauling harvest to Tanshelf,
brisket-deep in surgent Winwæd.

Layered in silts, the broke skulls of Penda
and thirty pagan Princes. Oswiu kept his vow;
twelve manors to the Church, and Ælffled
his daughter, to Hereteu, or Hampole.

Fowlers on the flash, netting godwits and ruff,
setting nooses for greylag and whooper.
Ilbert's men crowning-down lodges of beofor.
Hunters with lymers wading the reed-mere.

Luminous bullion of windfall crabs
clotting the stubblefield strandline,
poma bosci for Frenchman's cissera:
stuffed hogsheads boon of bowlegged children.

In the tavern at Went-Bridge, bad men count coin
and drain tankards; líð, the first æppelwin
of hærfesttid. Hroðgar called Roger,
Wilsige, Ælle, Johannes del Wode.

Murdrum hangs heavy, but thieves travel light.
Winwæd to Hatfield via Fenwick's dark lakes,
a day by punt and deer path. Hroðgar,
wolf's-head – fliema, utlaga.

Bloody Hatfield, Edwin gurning
from his heafodstocc. Cadwalla
sought slaughter of Engle and Seaxe,
drawing down heafonfyr, Whiteblade's justice.

Penda lopped on Winwæd's field,
and Æthelhere, his scab. Bold Oswui firing
Hroðgar's dreams – a gibbet of frogleg kings:
Curtmantle, Lionheart, Lackland.

Roger lurches to light in forester's green.
Companions behind him, belching
and farting, adjusting their weapons;
every day drinking and fighting.

Winwaedfeld opens before them like Breughel,
floods and flashes and servile ceorls, busy
at maître's bidding: de Laci's liege-man
Ralph de Paganel, usurper of Swein and Archil.

On stubbles by hreodfenn,
commotion of servants and horse:
Frethesenthe exquisite in gloves of white kid,
casting jack merlin at skylarks.

Her face is flushed like June's wild rose,
bosom and cheekbones high. Treasures
beneath her scarlet surcoat: coin-purse,
corset, stockings and skin. Jack bating off the fist.

Hunters and lymers, closing from reedmere;
hound voice, urgent shouts of men.
Hroðgar is vanished. Lark explodes in air.
The Lady swoons, her maidens squeal and sing –

alouette, gentille alouette,
alouette, je te plumerai.

The White Hart

Robertus Swynherd, of Elmsall-on-the-Hill,
smote Butcher's taxman on high road
twixt Pomfret and Danum.
Broadcast groats for stubblefield gleaners.

And fled his gret-headed gazehounds
to Lindholme's asylum, with Roben,
Iohannes and Alan of Barnysdale;
where they feasted on pikes and venison.

And flushed from birch scrub, a hart
of fifteen hands, bull-burly,
fathomed in tines, breasting Torne-spate
to Wood House and Hatfield beyond.

At Stane-Ford on Dun, Robert's
gret-headed gazehounds did him grapple
to ground; where *Grip* he skull-spiked,
divers tossed, and hobbled.

He forded to Fyselake and galloped
the ingas through Kirkhouse to Moss,
where Robert, with Roben and Willelmus
called *Red,* corralled him to Fenwick's mire.

Where houndis assailed him, and they let loose
arrows; but broadhead-pierced and ripped
of flesh, he leapt from Went's watter-world
and brok beyond Askern, to Campsall-on-the-stone.

On wold his ailing legs found strength,
ran horse and hounds ovr oppen field
to Wrang-brook, Upton, Elmsall-on-the-Hill;
where he frothed blood, and fell.

Exhaust on *street* twixt Pomfret
and Danum, the houndys held him at bay;
whereupon the Swynherd strode
through the melee, and slew him by sword.

In the White Hart that night was meat
and much drinking, Robertus and Roben,
Willelmus called *Red*; in their cups throwing silver
in rushes for children; where also they slept.

And woke to the point of Butcher's sword,
were dragged in chains to Pomfret;
where Robertus and Roben, Willelmus
called *Red*, were strung up on Beastfair gibbet.

For they took the King's coin and meat
from his chace and laid about his servants
with staves: the eve of St. Leonard.
Wild men came to Wentbridge by boat.

Iohannes and Hrothgar, Alan of Barnsdale;
many men of England. Across Hardwick moor
to Carleton, through Friar wood
to Beastfair; and cut them from the crows.

And laid them in their parish
at Ladychurch at Kirkby. Where Swein
& Arketil held carucates for geld
and the turned plow runs with blood.

Lindholme Asylum

A continual lake and a rondezvous of ye waters of ye
Rivers[...] Torne, Don, Ouse, Aire, Went, Idle, and Trent.
Abraham de la Pryme, Vicar of Thorne, 1699

Men hid in [...] islands, plundering and attacking those
who came their way.
Abingdon Chronicle

            Carrholme, Kilholme, Sandholme,
Axholme; dozens more
            juxta Danum, in the seas
between Scunthorpe, Gainsborough and Goole.
            Moraines and floodsands
humped on Humberhead's palaeolithic lake bed
            where seven rivers   faltered
and flattened to mere
            moating birch-scrub and oak-wood
in sedge-swamp, rush-quag and sinks
            of soaking sphagnum,
bog throbbing and quaking
            by bayou and blackbrook,
sky midged with teal and winter pintail,
            greylags squalling, belching deer.
Swein and Arkill, swan-breasting silts
            from gaping Hymbre to Lynd-holmr's beachhead,
clearing kjarr for svin and far and ko
            raising lang-hus in lang-thwaite, stot-fold.

Fen-wolf's watter-world, on fold falling
scheep and cow – French riding stræt
        to Lincoln, York. Keel-less coble
and pole-punt highways ferry fowles and fishes
        to Fennik and Crowle, men
stitched in skins, strapped axe and broadsword,
        announced
in drunk and brawling gutterals –
        YOU CAN GET FUCKING READY NOW.
Bill Bunting, Barnsley born-and-bred,
        brandishing bill-hook and Browning revolver,
eviscerate Frenchmen
        from Fisons and Drax, lickspittle NCC;
beofor, drain-wrecker, spirit of fen.

        HMP Lindholme. Barbed-wire
unregenerate stank. By Ten Acre Lake
        (red-neck, fire-eye)
a gibbet: the Bastard, his Sheriff, Cornelius Vermuyden –
        kicking off the beam.
Posing for photos,
        Hereward, Roben,
every Rougarou wolfshead from Lafayette County.
        Ekouté, mes amis; kréyol la Lwizyàn:
there are tigers in the fen, staghorned-sturgeons
        and prowling pikes,
boars clawed with knives and bears with banjos,
        ravening wolves, forked-beards and pit-boots,
sawn-off flat-cap, full-length duster –
        farming skunk, running shine
and bluetick coonhounds,
        brogued in segs and Blakey's horseshoes
melodion dancing on salted boards;
        on heads of cops, rats, scabs and nonces,
slash/dumped in sump, like poetry.

Tranmoor

Arnulf's torp, tran-mere
by holt-holmr and watter-ton.
Reed road to Danum,
Black Carr, Pissybeds, Spittlerush Lane.
Bitterns pointing the moon,
from flood-flat phragmites, oak stumps
proud of washed-out peat.
Torne-flash strand-line, acorn-flotsam,
wave-crests breaking
carp-cropped pastures,
eel-grassed submarine leys.

Straggling spearheads trompet
dawn-star, dark feather falling
Finn-mark to fen:
swing down barrel-belly,
broad-wing braking, hang-leg
bounce-down bustle on mere;
lunge-leap squalling
bashwing-brawling, thrown back
blood-badged woodpecker heads
bugle like loons
in waste's wide welkin.

Glazed from world in muffling
headphones, bus-stop sigh-stare
downpour dawn. Street-light
stair-rods, stiffer than bitterns.
Gullies gush and man-holes spurt,
bus-swerve brake-squeal crane-song:
all-a-bored. From Armthorpe,
oblivious – dutch-dyke,
grow-bags, windfarms, rapefield –
to Lakeside, Frenchgate, Junction 3,
Wheatley Retail Park.

Reintroduction of the English Wolf (2)

They denned in gorse at Bullcarr Mires,
moated in oilseed rape. Prowled tramline
slink-ways for hare and muntjac, rats and bank voles,
roadkill-roe – the bins at Blue Bell,
Fox & Hounds. The Express said howling
blew their cover, but the moochers knew,
and the farmers, high on their tractors:
the carp-lads on the flash, Eric running
long-dogs on the hill-top paddock (the blokes
from the rough shoot, the Wednesday ramblers,
the landlords at Blue Bell, Fox & Hounds).
Not a half-mile from playground, school and Co-op.
There was a meeting. Reasoned arguments/
demagogic assertion/uninformed hysteria.
Kids bolted to bedrooms, huddled round iPhones.
Vigilantes with pitbulls and baseball bats:
dreadlocked eco-Trots facing-off with Alliance;
Natural England consulting with stabjacket
TV cops. Dead dog on Harewood Lane,
half-eaten heifer at Hardwick – *a girl*
walking through woods to grandma's and never seen
again – pathologists pronounced [...] parvo
and blackleg. But the streets remained empty,
until folks got fed up and went out anyway.
On Springwatch the cubs proved cuter than meerkats
and the kill-by-kill inventory revealed:
rabbit, rabbit, bunny-bunny-hop-hop,
vox-popped locals running off at the mike,
providing BBC balance – *wonderful, a privilege/*
won't somebody think of the children.
Two wolves became eight and loped into autumn
through lead shot, poison and high beam headlights.
Sightings from Adwick, Askern, Goole; a trail
of ripped sheep and brown-trousered golfers.

New Year snows its constellations. Full moon
glazes streets with ice. Estates lit up
like touchscreens. On winter wheat by Bullcarr Mires,
wolves hackle and snarl in steaming darkness,
coupling, binding. Horse-henged hill-top,
pelting stars; Erik throws his head back, howls.

Brother Bear

Ego dormio et cor meum vigilat.
Cant.,V: 2

Ice fled him from fen
to folds of Burghwallis
where he brok barn
and killed a buck lamb.

Far baying of lymers
roused me from Psalter;
grating of claws
on my riveted door.

A square of light
in howling darkness;
stench of fear
and steaming death.

His yellow eyes met mine
and I thought of Elisha,
of Cuthbert and Francis –
and gave him sanctuary.

Matted in gore; lamb's-blood,
the entrails of mastiffs,
the steady seep
from gangrene bodkins.

Winter had him wasted.
His pelt hung off him
like a rug
on a clothes-horse.

At table we broke bread
together, lapping milk
and gnawing wheels of cheese.
He *was* famished.

I blessed him,
and he gave thanks,
bowing his head
to the plank of the table.

And I exhorted
our brother to kindle
his heart and covet
the fellowship of angels.

For all that is good
and holy, when fallen
from this world,
shall be taken into their orders.

Sudden snarling of hunters,
battering my door.
Hound voice, lovely,
lifting to heaven.

Æcerbot

His heart will be living in splendour and fire,
and marvellous music will exalt him. He will
pay no respect to any one, though he be thought
a bumpkin. In depths of his being there is praise
of God and jubilant song, and his praise bursts
out aloud; his sweet voice rises to heaven, and
the Divine Majesty delights to hear it.
Richard Rolle, *The Fire of Love*

I

Richard, rude raptured from Heaven
to haloed Hampole, hoist by indigent
dreaming. Dorter derelict, annihilate
ashlar, arcades and arches, fell.
Field folk faithless, vicious,
vexatious, venal with violence of lucre
and lies. Leys laid waste
and woodland withered, wildcat banished
with beaver and bristle-backed boar.
Brook bereft of barbel and grayling,
gravels greased green with Elmsall's
excreta, exudate of effluent plough.
Plucked of pear and peccant pippin,
pardes purged to ponied pasture, wrecked
of wryneck, rakish redstart, wrested
to the west. And whither the women? Mary,
Marjery, Margaret – *morte* – cloistered
in Cromwell's clay. And Richard said:

> *Barnsdale is fallen, fallen to wolf*
> *altars stripped, daughters dumped nude.*
> *In roofless precincts, dogs humping and howling*
> *licking blood from foot of the rood.*

Barnsdale dismembered, Priory sacked
and reft to Dudley's chests –
under the walnut, by banks of sweet Ea,
lips upon Marjery's breasts.

Barnsdale desarted, blighted by drought,
dry-well where once rang five springs.
Lucy aflighted, Bella bereft,
no more the nightingale sings.

Barnsdale is swallowed, alchemical wyrmes
eating earth, squirting-out gold.
Swine butchered from pannage and cattle
cut-off, sheep dragged-down in the fold.

Barnsdale racked on rood like our Lord
in England's broken land.
Yet body and blood, field, common and wood –
must stand.

So ride I will the Great North Road
from York to Canterbury,
our land and people to assize
in this bleak posterity.

II

Alien archpriests, accultured to Moloch,
missioned to manored and mannered. Mildness
masking mastery, mock meek militants,
manoeuvring for Mammon, murmuring for World.
Who walks in Wulstan's way,
with Wilgils and Wilfrid, Oswald whiteblade,
wilful, warlike, wise in lectionary
and lore? Who lists for law and jousts
for justice – Judgement for jobbers, jubilee
for Jack and Johanna? Journeyman saint

and simple sinner, from Sorbonne saved
by Saviour's soft and rinsing blood,
bull-bellowing from Barnsdale: from Bedale
to Bawtry, to Barnet and Blue Bell's sarsened
slopes, the soil is sick, fields
infertile, fouled of farming, reduced
to rental, real-estate. Emporious England,
embezzled, ectrotic – empery ebbing
away. And Richard said:

> *England is fallen, fallen to worms,*
> *Elizabeth's writhing gut;*
> *distended and swollen from touchscreen's troughs,*
> *fly-blown head-to-foot.*
>
> *Kent is cankered, cankered from Wen,*
> *plagued of capital's city;*
> *buboes of broker, gangrene of banker,*
> *chancre of planning committee.*
>
> *Wessex is wasted, to tractor and tank,*
> *to spray and shell and flail;*
> *Masters, squires and colonels prosper,*
> *evicted farmhands ail.*
>
> *Cumberland cumbered by clinker and slag,*
> *iodine 131;*
> *Blencathra's tooth-pulled Patterdales,*
> *rust-bit father's gun.*
>
> *Northumberland, fire-damp, cold with stone*
> *Cuthbert and collier dead;*
> *the cobles of the herring fleet, sunk*
> *off Longstone head.*
>
> *England ails, her fair field sick,*
> *thus Æcerbot I prepare;*
> *for increase of commonwealth and yield*
> *I make this healing prayer.*

III

On walnut warth, by waste of wimpled
wenches, did wonder-working Richard
altar raise from rapefield brash.
Shire's justice for snakes, swindlers
snatched from Skelbroke's mansions
and slaughtered on the stone. Spurt sluiced
to simmering basins, where phantoms feast and fume
to form in fair and familiar habit – four maids
of Mary's mansworn house, Margaret, Maud
and Margery, mistress Ysabel – mensal virgins,
vivid in valley, vested to England
and England's God. And Richard said:

> *Called from death by rude redeemer*
> *in holy name of Lady's Son,*
> *accept the call of Hampole's dreamer*
> *and work for England's remission.*
>
> *Fly from Barnsdale's wounded leys*
> *to the cardinal corners of the land*
> *where blood was spilled in rough melee*
> *of Anglian armies and Vik war-band.*
>
> > *Stainmoor's slopes aflame with gorse*
> > *wet with English blood and Norse.*
> >
> > *Maldon's cockled creeks and shoals*
> > *Brythnoth's head on Olaf's pole.*
> >
> > *Fulford fledged in flag and flax*
> > *ribbed in broadsword, battle-ax.*
> >
> > *Ethandun, sun swells the grain*
> > *from English blood, mud-mixed with Dane.*

Journey hence and from sacred sod
cut turve and gather worts of power,
bloods of beasts from field and wood
and baste the sward with blended flower.

To Barnsdale bring your pagan blot
that I may perform Æcerbot.

IV

To Frickley-in-the-fields, reformed to racked
All Saints, did Rolle repair for remedy.
First broke he boughs of burgeoned quick,
them coopering to rood, crossed-cudgels of Christ's
kerygmatists – armed, awaiting acre.
Then resorted to rood-rail, kneeling noon
into none, gnats knotting nets in the golden
grave-garth, grizzled under gean.
Garlick, goosegog, Good King Henry,
hawfinch husht in haws; grith's
grassed ground broken, grail
of black-muck bone-hoard bare, opened
earth's omphalos; Oswald's ossuary, of Olaf
and Offa, England's ostent dead.
Slit-light splayed in shafts cross
chancel, limed walls lucent, linen bright.
Bated-breath of bell and Bible,
batflit dust mote, transepts still.
Mansuete masspriest, meditating on missal,
on Mary's meek and militant maids –
Skögul, Skeggjöld, Sigrún, Skuld –
sanguined sod-bearers, sudden in sanctuary,
presenting sacred sward. And Ysabel said:

Sod of Stainmoor screes I bring
from Westmorland's high chase,
blood of Erik, Northern kings
asperged there on the waste.

At daybreak, honey, oil and yeast
cream from drystone field,
I tipped on turf to seek increase
and augment England's yield.

Spirits of nine herbs I smoked
in aromatic peat,
with beast-bloods gashed from pulsing throats
the ritual to complete.

Waybread, barley, bonewort, rye
mugwort, wheat and knap,
all-heal and agrimony
bear and boar and stag.

At Fulford, Maldon, Ethandune
these maids made similar rite,
at the rising of the Sun
to purge Englaland of blight.

So break bread, Richard, pour out wine
on Mary's sweet-tuft sod
and leaven land with love divine
come of the Son of God.

Trimmed altar, upturned turves;
Richard muck-Mass making. Wine and wafer,
wattered on wrang-root; wounded
worm-worts, clutching rubble:

> *Wexe and gemænigfealda and gefylle þas eorðan,*
> *in Nomine Patris, et Filii, et Spiritus Sancti, sit benedicte.*

Sod-sired and soil-infused
with Spirit, slung in surpliced loam, did Dick
and damsels ere dusk-dark gather
by graveyard's grafted earth. By grace
of God and gramarye, good Richard
raised each rowan-wrought rood
and rammed them roughly in gaping ground:

Crux Matthaeus, crux Marcus,
crux Lucas, crux sanctus Iohannes.

Then laid our ladies on Jesse's branch
the burgeoning baize of England's balm,
bred of battlefield's blood.

Gemænigfealda and gefylle, in nomine Patris,
thrice three-times chanted
God's sod-soiled shield maids,
mooning sunset, singing:

> *Sun of the East, burn blood in my face*
> *light this land with life*
> *in Jesu's name, inflame increase,*
> *Mary, womb and wife.*
>
> *Let wheat-field bloom with leavened loaves*
> *and bere-field belch with beer*
> *foam of wold-sheep clot the droves*
> *at table, kine-milk, beef of steer.*
>
> *Let orchards bow, infest with fruit*
> *swine swarm across the pannage*
> *let virgins' bellies rise with loot*
> *of Mayday's stolen marriage.*
>
> *Bring bounty's blessing to our land*
> *and rinse the shires of dearth*
> *swill of mighty, proud and grand*
> *manuring England's earth.*

V

Damsels dancing like fitches in dusky fire-glow,
in lithe and limber litany to Lord.
Night-crow's Kyrie, rawping from rag-flagged
bell-tower, toppling tombstones, raising dead.
Dogstar darkness, dimmed the dreaming welkin;
wenches withered from Word to wyrd,
dying to the light. Lantern longshanks
stubblefield striding, ghostly Shire team
priested to plough. Plague pit paupers,
proud of parish, parading behind him,
pockets exploding with seed. Brace bit
plough beam, bored above mouldboard –
Patris, Filii,Spiritus Sancti – slaked
sheepsalve, salt and fecund fennel,
fragrant frankincense. Freighted stallions
thrusting forward, unfurling furrow; almseed
slathered in share-sharked sod,
gushed of gape in plough beam's glistening wood.
Nine times did Rolle's phantom plough
circle All Saint's earth – and Richard cwæþ:

> *Erce, Erce, Erce,   eorþan modor,*
> *geunne þe se alwalda   ece drihten,*
> *æcera wexendra   and wridendra,*
> *eacniendra   and elniendra,*
>
> *sceafta hehra,   scirra wæstma,*
> *and þæra bradan   berewæstma*
> *and þæra hwitan   hwætewæstma,*
> *and ealra   eorþan wæstma.*

Beggars barney in plough wake, bestial
with beer; seed spurting from split lips,
splayed cheekbones and shiners; horseshit
housel, broadcast body and blood. Leavened
to loam-loaf and folded in furrow,
four flours of Frickley's fields, yeasting
yokel and yeoman, future's flea-bit fyrd:

> Let salmon surge in Went and Skel
> hart leap in Hampull wood
> boar rip the brake at Holywell
> bull-bellow brawl from Stubbs.
>
> Cow-cream gush like thunder-hole
> sheep-fleece shed like snake
> every mare be twinned of foal
> with piglets sow-wombs quake.
>
> Autumn apples fall like rain
> cobnuts crunch like snails
> bean-pods swell and snap the cane
> tankards froth with ales.
>
> Barley spike like wolfhide
> wheat stand straight as spear
> oat-heads hiss like Humber tide
> rye bend with burthened ear.
>
> God of England's life and land
> hear her restless dead.
> On blood and muck we make our stand,
> her soft-soil's blooming redd.

* * *

Bronze horizon, mist-rag tilth. Heron
on headland, rat-hung gullet. Hound-voice,
distant. Hare sits up from earth. And cleans
her ears. Spitting rain. Sky folds
like a black-back's wing. Rain.

Ricardo heremita

Who set the wild asse free? His tent is the salty earth.
Joob: 39:5-6

The fourfold root of perfect freedom:
accept grace, fight flesh, live lonely, long for bliss.
Elect, I sin not, even in my sinning.
Noon-day demons cast down cross and tempt me
to tossing; I prate in hall for meats and wine,
suck tits of maids and poke their holes. I burn.
Honey in tree-holes, counterpoint cuckoo
and throbbing of bees. Uncut topaz,
muck-plucked Dog-bright diamond; polished, I am dull,
and plod like haulier's gelded donkey,
bray like Father's gelded priests. Sit with me.
Burn candles, sweet incense. Join me in song.

Afterword

Richard Rolle (1300?-1349) was born at Thornton Dale near Pickering in the North Riding of Yorkshire, a son of the 'small householder' William Rolle. By the efforts of his parents he was sent to school and he later went to Oxford under the patronage of Thomas Neville, Archdeacon of Durham. However, disillusioned by the worldliness of the University, he returned to Yorkshire, where he adopted the eremitical life. Although Rolle subsequently studied at the Sorbonne, and was probably ordained, his ministry was essentially a charismatic one in that he does not seem to have been affiliated with any monastic or church order.

In the early stages of his eremitical career, Rolle relied on the patronage of wealthy landed families and seems to have attracted criticism that his lifestyle was insufficiently ascetic, in that he enjoyed the table and the company of women a little too much. He alludes to and defends himself against these accusations in his works. The character of Rolle's spiritual writings, with their earthy, emotional and indisputably erotic spirituality also seems to have drawn criticism from more orthodox religious (including Walter Hilton and the author of the *Cloud of Unknowing*).

By the 1340s (at the latest), Rolle had moved to the West Riding and was attached to the Cistercian nunnery at Hampole, on the high toby between Doncaster and Pontefract in the heart of Robin Hood's Barnsdale. Living in 'a shack in the fields', he was confessor and spiritual advisor to the nuns until his death (probably of the plague), in 1349.

At Hampole, Rolle became particularly close to a young nun named Margaret of Kirkby. He became Margaret's spiritual director and seems to have cured her of an epilepsy-like condition, promising her that she would not experience the symptoms again as long as he lived. His advice to 'Dame

Margaret' survives in his epistle, *The Form of Living* and other writings. Rolle's relationship with Margaret was close and passionate and his writings allude to occasions when he was chided by her for over familiarity.

In 1348 Margaret was enclosed as an anchoress in a cell attached to the parish church at Ainderby Steeple in the North Riding. However, sometime during 1349 she was once more affected by 'seizures' – and thus became certain of Rolle's death. This being confirmed to her, she returned to Hampole and re-joined the convent as a nun. Over the next several decades Margaret played an important role in establishing Richard's cult, which was based on the shrine built over his grave in the Priory chapel by one 'Paterfamilias Rogerus'. Soon after Richard's death, miracles began to be attributed to him and pilgrims came from across the three Ridings (and beyond) to pray and burn candles at his tomb. Rolle grew in posthumous renown and his works were published throughout Europe. In the late fourteenth century the nuns of Hampole commissioned and published the *Officium et Miracula de Sancto Ricardo* (a church service made up of liturgical elements, prayers, encomia and accounts of Richard's miracles) in anticipation of his canonisation. However, despite his European celebrity, Rolle was never officially made a Saint. It is probable that his lack of affiliation, combined with his unorthodox spirituality and the hints of scandal in his life, led to this failure.

Despite this, Rolle remained 'Saint Richard' in vernacular Catholicism until Henry VIII's caesaro-papist privatisation and expropriation of the church. On the nineteenth of November, 1539, Hampole Priory was 'surrendered' and claimed by John Dudley, Duke of Northumberland. In the decades that followed, the Priory and its chapel were dismantled and the cult of Richard Rolle was extirpated along with the vibrant folk traditions of English Catholicism. Richard's shrine now lies somewhere under the village green, where his links with the Abbey are marked by a modest plaque.

What survive of Rolle are his writings. *Incendium Amoris* (written in Latin, but translated into English as *The Fire of Love* by Richard Misyn as early as 1435) is perhaps the best exemplification of his fervent mysticism – with its emphatic focus on the Holy Name, the Five Wounds and his characteristic meditational practice of 'sitting', leading to religious experiences characterised by 'heat, sweetness and song'. Epistles such as *Ego Dormio*, *The Commandment* and the *Rule for Living* testify to not only to Rolle's spiritual insight, but his ongoing struggle against an irresistible carnality, as he strove to fulfil the expectations of the eremitical life. His typically idiosyncratic translation of the Psalms is one of the earliest mediaeval renderings of a Biblical book into English, and of course, his lyrics are among the first works of 'Middle English'. *The English Writings of Richard Rolle, Hermit of Hampole* (1931), edited by Hope Emily Allen and Clifton Wolter's *The Fire of Love* (1972) are good places to start for those interested.

Notes

Old Street
Old Street is Lound Lane, the Brodsworth-to-Hampole section of an ancient Iron Age/Roman road – the location of visions, apparitions and dreams. 'Pound's phantom hell hounds' were psychically perceived accompanying Ezra by W.B. Yeats, whose own daemon was the spirit of the Berber diplomat 'Leo Africanus'. The 'midnight dog-fox' belongs to Ted Hughes.

Catweazle
Catweazle was a time-travelling 11th century wizard in the eponymous 1970 LWT children's TV programme. 'Stromatolite reef'– the Magnesian limestone that underlies Barnsdale includes a fossilised reef which is occasionally exposed at the surface. 'Asiotic'– pertaining to the long-eared owl. The various 'balks' in 'Officium'– Love, Broad, Badger/Lenny – are footpaths between Hampole and Hooton Pagnell. Yommer, Malc and Joey are moochers of my acquaintance. 'Fishponds Wood' at nearby Bilham is a locus of 'anti-social behaviour', according to warning posters put up by South Yorkshire Police. 'Richard and Margret' are Richard Rolle and Margaret of Kyrkeby.

Jerusalem
Ordnance Survey 'Pathfinder' maps reveal the route of Old Street as proceeding from the Don ford at Strafford Sands in Conisborough to Pontefract ('Tanshelf'). 'Rat Hall' is a farm near Brodsworth; 'Watlynge Street' is the nearby Great North Road. 'Endymion non-scripta' is the scientific name for the bluebell.

Bloen
'Bloen' is a Romany word connoting a regular, but casual female sexual partner. 'Badger Balk' was the only place in Bilham parish where itinerants ('badgers') had the right to graze their horses. 'The Ghost of a Flea' is the spirit of violence Blake saw at a séance at his friend John Varley's house in 1819, and subsequently painted.

Ostentio Vulnerum
Ostentio vulnerum means 'display of the wounds'. 'Lucy' and 'Margot' (de Luterel) were nuns at Hampole Priory in the 14th century. 'Aske' is Robert Aske, the leader of the Pilgrimage of Grace, which in 1536 passed through Hampole on Watlynge Street, under the banner of the Five Wounds of Christ.

Sweoster
'Sweoster' is the Old English word for sister; my sister Jayne and her family lived at Hampole for a time in the 1990s. The 'Cromwell' referred to is Thomas, the destroyer of the Church.

Pastoral
The italic phrase is from Psalm 50.10. Richard commented on Margaret of Kyrkeby's 'gret papys' in chapter twelve of his *Incendium Amoris*.

Rapture
Richard dwelt and wrote in a 'shack in the fields'. 'Blæc' is the name given to the ink used by mediaeval scribes. 'Rum, ram, raf' is how Northerners rhyme, according to Chaucer's *The Reeve's Tale*.

To Mega Therion
'To Mega Therion' is 'the Great Beast' described in the Book of Revelation. 'Venite exultemus domino' ('Come let us praise the Lord') is the incipit of Psalm 95, the invitatory sung daily before Matins. 'None' is the ninth hour, three in the afternoon.

Banquet of Virgins
The Ea beck runs through Hampole to the river Don.

The harpe, and the voice of a Psalme
The final line is from Psalm 98.1, Rolle's rendering from his *Commentary on the Psalter*.

Pilgrimage of Grace
'Megiddo' is the city of Armaggedon. 'Golgonooza' is Blake's city of fourfold vision. A 'Zetor' is a brand of tractor.

Miracula

The poems in this section describe miracles attributed to Rolle in the *Officium et Miracula*, although some are transfigured to a more modern period.

Paterfamilias Rogerus, of Hampole

Rogerus financed the building of Richard's shrine at Hampole Priory and was saved from being crushed during the shrine's construction by the Saint's supernatural intervention.

Hugo of Fyselake

Hugo was restored to life after drowning when his parents burned a candle the size and weight of their son before Richard's shrine.

Iohanna of Sprotborough

Iohanna was similarly revivified after drowning.

Iohannes of Sutton

Iohannes had his sight restored after praying at Richard's shrine.

Isabella of Auston

Isabella was also cured of blindness by the Saint's intervention. A 'moon-pie' is the Romany name for a glaucous wall-eye.

The Paralytic of Wrangbroke

The unamed paralytic was able to walk after the Saint miraculously appeared to her in her home.

Thomas of Morehows

Thomas was cured of a fever after his parents burned a two-pound candle at Richard's shrine.

Willelmus filius Radulphi

Willelmus was bitten by an adder but was saved from death by the Saint's intervention after his parents prayed at his tomb.

Bodleian MS Rawlinson D. 913

These five poems are modelled on the Middle English lyrics 'I syng of a mayden', 'I have a yong suster', 'Maiden in the mor lay, 'Foweles in the frith' and 'Adam lay ybounden', each fortuitously preserved in the MS of the sequence title.

Paul and Laura Mandragora

'Puppette' and 'mammette' were the names given to the male and female amulet-figurines made from mandrake root by mediaeval cunning-men.

The Banishing Ritual of the Pentagram

In (I) the unravelling of creation is explored with help from the Genesis creation story, the legend of the Golem, Gnosticism, the allegory of Adam Kadmon and *Gawain & the Green Knight*. The Golem is activated by placing of the word אמת (truth) in his mouth and deactivated by removing the letter aleph (א) from the word, turning truth to מת (death). Removing the aleph from the word אדם (man) gives the word דם (blood). In (II) the pentagram is inverted and thus becomes evil, an emblem of black magic and the laissez-faire narcissism that flows from that. 'Vas nefandum' – the 'heinous vessel', Aleister Crowley's preferred mode of congress. In (III) 'Adam Weishaupt' is the founder of the Illuminati and 'Doctor Yakub' is the mad scientist who created the devilish white race in a laboratory experiment in Nation of Islam aetiology. 'Cheetah' is the tame chimpanzee from the Tarzan films. In (IV) the Golem myth is revisited. The Hebrew question (Ma enosh?/What is a man?) is quoted from Psalm 8:4 and is regarded by Biblical scholar John Rogerson as the 'central question of Old Testament theology'. The final verse references the executions that followed the Spartacus rebellions in Rome (71 BC) and Berlin (1919 AD).

Scandalum Cruces

'William Warham' was Archbishop of Canterbury, 1503-32. He attempted to resist Henry VIII's coup against the church. Henry 'Doubleday' was a pioneer of organic farming and founded the Soil Association. 'Phil Smith' was head of Religious Studies at

Maltby Comprehensive School. *On the Fourfold Root of the Principle of Sufficient Reason* was the title of Arthur Schopenhauer's doctoral thesis. A 'kraker' is a corncrake. 'Two-thousand-eight-hundred-and-sixty-five frankly impossible things': the enumerated propositions of the Catechism of the Catholic Church. 'Pete Bucknall' was right-back for the Travellers F.C. during the 1990s and remains a stalwart of the annual July trip to York Races.

Wealhhnutu

A walnut tree grows across the Ea beck from the site of Hampole Priory, presumably a survivor (or a descendant of a survivor), from the Priory gardens. 'Tafod' is a Welsh word meaning 'tongue'. The Old English quote beginning *'Engle and Seaxe'* is taken from *The Battle of Brunanburh*. 'Auster', 'Vaturus' and 'Aquila' are favourite winds. 'Dave Harcombe', the doyen of the working-terrier-man, publishes the magazine *Earth Dog, Running Dog*. 'Lucy de Luterel' was a nun of Hampole in the fourteenth century.

Wesyll

The only creature capable of slaying the basilisk, as Richard explains in his commentary on Psalm XC: 13.

Little Saint Hugh

The ballad that opens the piece is based on the folk song 'Little Sir Hugh' and its variants. The 'Lexinton brothers', including Bishop Henry, benefitted from the events following the Lincoln blood libel and probably encouraged or organised it. 'The Lateran Palace' (the Vatican) taught toleration of Jews on the grounds that scripture required their conversion as a precondition of the Second Coming. 'tennis courts at Minsthorpe' refers to an incident in a 1978 student strike at that West Yorkshire High School. (Jack) 'smethhurst' played a racist northerner in the 1970s ethnic-mismatch TV comedy *Love Thy Neighbour*. 'Mosley' is Oswald, founder of the British Union of Fascists. 'jamie jones' (Buchanan) of Leeds Rhinos cracked wise to an audience of Super League scholars at the time of the 2011 riots. *'I found an old stocking...'* was a borstal ballad sung by kids on South Kirkby's Wimpey Estate during the 1970s. Ezra Pound's 'Canto LII' is repeatedly referenced in the sections that begin, 'Grain swells in fragrant' and 'poor yitts pay Stinkschuld's price'. 'Abundance of nature' – Pound argued that the only valid interest was that based on natural increase. 'George-hill' is where the Diggers dug. 'Leopold of Siena', Pound's exemplary banker, founded the Monte de Paschei bank, which never charged more than 5% interest and returned its profits to 'the people' every five years, apparently. 'Nithhogg' is the dragon in Norse mythology that gnaws at the roots of Yggdrasil, the World Tree. Shylock frequented the 'Rialto' in the *Merchant of Venice*. T.S. Eliot developed Shakespeare's anti-Semitic caricature in his 'Burbank with a Baedeker: Bleinstein with a Cigar', from which the phrase 'underneath the lot' is appropriated. In the *Cantos*, Pound referred to Jews as 'neschek', a mistransliteration of the Hebrew נֶשֶׁךְ ('naschak' – literally, 'biter'), referring to the stereotypically Jewish practice of extracting extortionate interest. 'Not narrowly racialist' is critic William Cookson's disingenuous comment on the anti-Semitism of 'Canto LII' in his *A Guide to the Cantos of Ezra Pound*. [Philip] Sassoon was a member of the fabulously wealthy Rothschild family who went on to a career in Government despite the brutal anti-Semitism he experienced at Eton, Oxford and elsewhere. 'Ikey Solomon' was a cockney fence of the first half of the 19th century and the model for Dickens's Fagin. The 'saccarium Aaronis' was a department of the Exchequer set up by Henry II in 1185 to track down the fabulous wealth of Aaron of Lincoln, which escheated to the Crown on the his death. Much of this wealth was frittered on Richard I's crusades or was lost in the North Sea when John's treasury, en route to Bishop's Lynn, was swamped by incoming tides on the mudflats of the Wash. A 'tallage' was a special tax, applied at the Monarch's whim. Jews were repeatedly subjected to crippling tallages by a succession of English kings prior to their expulsion from England by Edward I in 1290. 'D.D. Kaminsky' is Danny Kaye. Excerpts of three songs from Charles Vidor's 1952 film *Hans Christian Anderson*, in which Kaye played the starring role, are quoted in this section. The 'Wannsee' conference of 20th January, 1942 set in motion the decisive phase of the Final Solution. The 1492 'Alhambra decree' expelled the Jews from Spain. Chişinău was the site of anti-Jewish pogroms in 1903 and 1905. The 'Maccabi' beer company sponsors a number of Israeli football teams. 'Gazza' is Geordie savant Paul Gascoigne, the most talented English footballer of the modern period. The footballers named in the final section are either Jewish or have strong Jewish links. Ardiles, Hoddle, Kluivert and Cruijff played for the 'Jewish clubs', Spurs and Ajax. The Israelis 'Rocket' Ronnie Rosenthal and Avi Cohen played for Liverpool, as did the Ukranian Andriy Voronin. Sjaak Swart played for Ajax and Juan Pablo Sorin was an Argentinian international. Jeff Agoos played for D.C. United and represented the U.S.A. 'Sheol' is the name given to the underworld in the Hebrew Bible. A 'Surridge Cobbler' was a brand of football, used in the professional game until the 1980s. In the final verse, a popular English football chant is conflated with an anti-Semitic song chanted by Feyenoord ultras at their Ajax rivals.

Je te plumerai
This poem is set at the edge of the Yorkshire fen in the early fourteenth century, near to the site of the battle of Windwaedfield (655AD), at which Oswy's Northumbrian forces defeated Penda of Mercia and his allies. 'Frethesenthe' was a daughter of William Paynell of Hooton Pagnell and the wife of Geofrey de Luterel, who succeeded to Paynell's manor by marrying her. The 'skylark' was the traditional quarry of the lady's falcon, the 'jack merlin'.

The White Hart
The White Hart was an ancient coaching inn at North Elmsall on the Wakefield branch of the Great North Road, a haunt of the notorious highwayman John Nevison and a long line of proud and bloody men before and after him. 'Lindholme' is a low island in the fen of Hatfield Waste. The Yorkshire Danes 'Swein & Arketil' held land in the general area of the poem's setting until the Norman annexation. The poem is set in 1379, in which year John of Gaunt ('Butcher') levied the second Poll Tax (even the poorest had to pay a groat) on behalf of the child-king Richard II.

Lindholme Asylum
During the 1970s and 1980s William Bunting led an uncompromising campaign against Fisons Ltd, the Nature Conservancy Council and Doncaster local authority, who between them were intent on destroying Thorne and Hatfield moors – the largest remaining raised bogs in lowland England – by strip-mining peat, developing the sites as quarries and landfills and by plans to build an airport. The team of proto-eco-warriors led by Bunting were known as 'Bunting's Beavers', as every weekend they would dam and otherwise destroy the drains and canals that were being dug by engineers to drain the bog. *'Ekouté, mes amis; kréyol la Lwizyàn'* – the fen folk were Anglo-Danish Cajuns.

Tranmoor
An area of land at the edge of the former Yorkshire fen, near Armthorpe, Doncaster. 'Trana' is Old Norse for 'crane'.

Æcerbot
The Old English charm Æcerbot ('Field Remedy') is an ancient and elaborate rite designed to restore fertility to a field. A version of the original can be found in Cockayne's, *Leechdoms, Wortcunning, and Starcraft of Early England.* In this re-imagining, Richard Rolle *redivivus* is imagined conducting the rite for the nation. Several quotations from the rite are embedded in the poem.

Acknowledgements

'Reintroduction of the English Wolf (1)' was published in *The Don & Dearne, 2015*. 'I syng of a lad', 'Wulf on weald', 'I have a yong whippet', 'Were in weald lay' and 'Richard lay a-weeping' were published in *The North*. 'Paul and Laura Mandragora' was published in *Butcher's Dog*. 'Wealhhnutu' was published in *Ambit*. 'The White Hart', 'Eofor' and 'Hugo of Fyselake' were published in *The Poetry Review*. 'Lindholme Asylum' was published in *Magma*. 'Reintroduction of the English Wolf (2)' was published in *The Dark Horse*. 'Little Saint Hugh' was commissioned by Radio 3's *The Verb* and was recorded and broadcast in November 2016. *Incendium Amoris* was completed with the help of a Northern Writers' Award.